The Digital Startup Playbook

Your First Steps to Online Success

C. M. Shepherd

Table of Contents

Disclaimer	1
Welcome to Your Entrepreneurial Adventure	3
Starting Smart: How Financial Clarity Fuels Business Success	6
Naming Your Space: Creating a Domain That Reflects Your Vision	8
Simplified Website Creation: How to Build a Professional Site with User-Friendly Tools	16
How to Create a Website Without Knowing Any Code	16
Choose the Right Website Builder	16
AI your Website & Content Creator	18
Pro tip:	19
The Phone Service, CRM, and the Gmail Mirage: Unveiling the Secrets to Business Success	20
The Business Line	20
THE CRM: Your Secret Weapon for Success	22
How the CRM will organize your business	22
Limitations of a Free CRM	24
Popular Free CRM Options	25
Free Email vs Paid Email: The Limitations of Free Gmail for Business Use	26
Maximizing Social Media for Sales and Relationships	30
Defining Your Business Goals	30
Researching Your Audience	31

Choosing Platforms for Selling	32
Choosing Platforms for Relationship Building	33
Tailoring Your Content to the Platform	34
Measuring Performance and Adjusting	34
Audience Research Breakdown for Social Media	35
Leveraging Social Media Quickly	36
Getting up to speed	36
Automating your post	37
Scaling Your Business with Affiliate Marketing: A Low-Cost Strategy	39
How Affiliate Marketing Can Complement Your Business	39
Selecting the Right Affiliate Programs and Promoting Offers on Various Platforms	41
Building Trust & Leading	42
Your Business Blueprint: Key Steps for Online Success	48
Final Thoughts and Gratitude	54

Disclaimer

The information presented in *The Digital Startup Playbook: Your First Steps to Online Success* is provided only for educational and informational purposes only. While every effort has been made to ensure the accuracy of the content, the author makes no representation or warranty regarding the completeness, accuracy, reliability, or suitability of the advice for your specific circumstances.

Starting and running a business involves risks, and the success of any venture depends on numerous factors, including your personal effort, business environment, and market conditions. The strategies and suggestions outlined in this book are based on the author's experience and research, but individual results may vary.

Please note that subscription services, software, and applications mentioned in this book may have been changed, updated, or discontinued since the publication date. Readers are encouraged to verify the current terms, pricing, and availability of any services referenced.

This book does not constitute professional, legal, financial, or business advice. Readers are encouraged to consult with qualified professionals, such as attorneys, accountants, or business advisors, before making significant business decisions or investments.

The author and publisher are not responsible for any losses, damages, or adverse outcomes that may arise from the use of the information in this book.

Welcome to Your Entrepreneurial Adventure

Are you ready to start your business but feel held back by a lack of funds? I've been there, and let me tell you—it's possible! There is no one way to start a business. The first step is being clear about your vision.

When I started, I invested in an online class that claimed to hold the key to entrepreneurial gold. She called it a business in a box. She initially claimed it was the only class I needed. Little did I know, I was about to be tossed onto a rollercoaster ride of debt and confusion, leaving me more lost than a squirrel in rush-hour traffic.

I'm not one to point fingers, but this "guru" had a natural talent for convincing me to spend money I didn't have. It felt like I was stuck in an endless loop of "buy this" and "subscribe to that," and then I could get over the hurdle. All while my business didn't make a single dime.

Determined to save my business—and my sanity—I sought advice on how to start a company the "right" way. I read books and tapped into state and federal resources, trying to piece things together. While I found plenty of information, much of it painted an unrealistic picture: one that required $10,000 or more and a flawless business plan to succeed. But that wasn't my reality. I had debt, good credit, and a dream of earning more than my current job allowed. So, I was left with a question: should I stop now or keep pushing forward?

It would've been easy to give up and complain about how unfair it was. But here's the thing—I don't walk away from a challenge. I began rebuilding and reworking my business; I wanted to share what I had learned and wish someone had told me.

You don't need a fat wallet or a perfect business plan to succeed. Today's technology has budget-friendly tools and services to help you build a thriving business without breaking the bank. You only need a little know-how, some creativity, and a dash of determination.

So, buckle up, fellow maverick entrepreneur. Together, we will flip the script on those discouraging statistics and show the world that you can succeed even when your piggy bank is squealing for mercy. The adventure starts now!

Your Fellow Maverick,

C. M. Shepherd

Starting Smart: How Financial Clarity Fuels Business Success

Let's discuss your budget. I know it's uncomfortable —like ripping off a bandaid—but it's necessary.

We'll start by reviewing your current expenses. You might feel hesitant, maybe even afraid, of what you'll uncover. Why? Because you might feel embarrassed that things haven't been managed perfectly. But here's the truth: don't be. Everyone makes mistakes, and what's important now is learning from them and making changes.

So, let's get those expenses itemized. Write down your household spending without overthinking it— get it all on paper. Before you dive into business, it's crucial to have a clear understanding of your financial situation. Know exactly where you stand, whether you're starting from zero or even in a negative. What matters is that you begin with clarity.

A wise woman once told me, "It's not about where you start; it's about where you finish." If you're worried you won't like what you see, decide now that you will change it. This exercise aims to understand your starting point so you can begin moving forward.

I want to emphasize that you should not spend money you don't have. If you think your need is outside your budget, find something else to replace it. Now, this is not always a plausible solution, but most of the time, it is. I cringe whenever a salesperson tries to persuade me to buy a big-ticket solution and tells me how easily a business will pay for its service with a certain amount of sales. I am not making my debt for me or my company. I plan my purchases after my sales, not before.

Once you have a clear picture of your financial landscape, you can start making smarter decisions about your business. Knowing your limits doesn't hold you back; it empowers you to prioritize, plan, and allocate resources effectively. By understanding what you're working with, you can take confident steps toward building your business in a way that aligns with your vision and financial reality.

Naming Your Space: Creating a Domain That Reflects Your Vision

Onward you go, let's start with selecting an effective domain name. Think of it as your digital address and how it represents your brand online. The right domain name can significantly impact your business's visibility and credibility, making it easier for potential customers to find and remember you. Choosing a memorable, easy-to-spell domain name that reflects your brand or purpose is important.

It's time to find your address on the Internet. The first thing to do is create your domain name. I recommend making 10-20 variations of the name. There are domain extensions, such as ".com," ".org," and country-specific options. Understanding domain extensions' unique advantages and disadvantages will assist you in choosing the right one. Be mindful of the extension you choose.

A domain name extension, also known as a top-level domain (TLD), is the part of a web address that comes after the domain name. Here are some of the more common extensions:

- **.com** : The most popular TLD, derived from the word "commercial."
- **.net:** Originally used for websites about networks.
- **.org:** Used for nonprofit organizations.
- **.edu** : Typically used for educational institutions.
- **.biz** : For business, commerce, or trade.
- **.tech** : Embrace innovation from technology with a .tech domain.
- **.io:** Often associated with "input/output," which resonates with tech-savvy audiences and companies focused on software, hardware, and IT solutions
- **.art:** Unleash your creativity with a .art domain.
- **.photography** : Showcase your visual artistry with a .photography domain.
- **.design** : This can help you to express your creativity through a .design domain.

- **.travel:** You can embark on a digital journey with a .travel domain.

- **.info:** A generic top-level domain (gTLD) for websites providing information or general online content. The extension is short for "information" and is a popular choice for various websites, including blogs, news sites, and educational resources.

- **.guru:** The .guru domain extension is a distinctive and evocative TLD that has gained traction for individuals, experts, and businesses looking to establish themselves as authorities in their respective fields. It has become a go-to choice for personal branding and consulting services, offering a memorable and marketable online presence.

When choosing a domain extension, consider the purpose of your website, as well as your target audience and market. Different extensions convey different messages. For instance, .com is versatile and globally recognized, .org is associated with nonprofits, and tech startups often opt for .io.

Think about your brand identity. Your domain name, including its extension, is crucial in shaping your brand. Ensure that the extension aligns with your brand and reflects the image you want to project.

Consider the availability of your desired domain name under the extension you want. Some extensions might be crowded and have limited availability, while others offer a more comprehensive selection of available names.

While domain extensions don't directly impact SEO, using a relevant and trustworthy extension can contribute to your website's credibility. Users are likelier to trust and click on sites with .com or .org extensions.

Stay informed about current market trends and popular domain extensions. What's popular today may change, so aligning with current trends can help your website appear more relevant to users.

Conduct competitor analysis to research your competitors' domain extensions. Consider whether you want to follow a similar pattern or differentiate yourself in the market.

Remember, selecting the right domain extension requires thoughtful consideration. By considering your website's purpose, target audience, brand identity, geographic relevance, availability, SEO impact, budget, market trends, and competitor analysis, you can choose a domain extension that confidently represents your brand and resonates with your audience.

First and foremost, a memorable domain name enhances the chances of visitors returning to your site. For example, if you run a pet grooming service, a name like **"PetGroomingPros.com** indicates what your business offers while being easy to remember. But what if it is taken and PetGroomingPros.com is available instead? I would recommend researching that business. Find out if the company is well established and if it is a potential competitor. If it is a competitor, then consider another domain because the website is established and is bound to confuse potential customers and could take business from you. Work on a unique name.

Next, ease of spelling is vital. Complicated or ambiguous spellings could lead potential visitors to misspell your URL, driving them away from your site. For instance, avoid names like " **XclsvDesigns.com,** " which may be confused with alternative spellings. Choose something simple and intuitive to avoid these pitfalls.

Reflecting your brand or purpose in the domain name not only aids memorability but also builds trust and credibility. For instance, a home-based bakery might choose "

SweetHomemadeTreats.com " to immediately inform visitors about the nature of the business. This clarity fosters trust and attracts the right audience.

Different domain extensions serve various purposes and audiences. The most common extension, ".com," is widely recognized and trusted, making it a safe choice for most businesses. However, other extensions like ".org" and ".net" can also be effective depending on the nature of your business. For instance, ".org" is often associated with nonprofits and organizations, adding an aura of credibility for such entities.

While ".com" is preferable due to its familiarity and trustworthiness, securing other extensions can protect your brand from competitors who might try to use them. For example, owning "YourBrand.org" and "YourBrand.net" alongside "YourBrand.com" ensures that visitors find your site even if they mistakenly use a different extension.

When selecting a solid domain name, longevity should also be a consideration. Ideally, choose a name you'll stick with over the long term because changing your domain later can confuse customers and negatively impact your search engine rankings. An older, stable domain builds authority over time, improving SEO performance.

Avoid using numbers, hyphens, or special characters in your domain name. These elements complicate the URL's typing process and can easily lead to errors. For instance, **"Best-Cake-Shop-123.com** " is more complicated to remember and prone to typographical mistakes than "BestCakeShop.com."

When choosing a domain name, consider future growth or expansion potential. Ensure the name remains relevant and adaptable as your business evolves. If you start as a local business but plan to expand globally, select a name that won't limit your future audience's reach.

Register your domain name with a trusted domain registrar to secure and prevent others from claiming it. Reputable registrars provide additional services like privacy protection, renewal management, and customer support, which are vital for maintaining your domain's integrity.

Cost tip: Once you find the available domain, shop for the best price. One company will charge $.99, while another will charge $29.99. Domain registers and runs sales like every other company, competing for your business.

You cannot buy a domain name outright; you lease it a year at a time. If you can find a reasonable price, you can lease it for multiple years in advance, saving you a nice chunk of cash. Another thing to consider is that some domain providers will provide email addresses with the domain.

Simplified Website Creation: How to Build a Professional Site with User-Friendly Tools

How to Create a Website Without Knowing Any Code

Creating a website is easier than ever. Thanks to technological advancements, many user-friendly platforms allow anyone to build a professional-looking website quickly and easily. This guide will walk you through designing your website without creating any code.

Choose the Right Website Builder

The first step is to choose a website builder that suits your needs. Website builders allow you to design, customize, and manage a website without knowing how to code. Some of the most popular website builders include:

- **Wix** : Known for its drag-and-drop simplicity, Wix offers a wide range of templates and customization options.

- **Hostinger** : Has created AI technology that will build your website within minutes.

- **Squarespace** : Famous for its beautifully designed templates, Squarespace is an excellent option for creatives and businesses that want a sleek, modern look.

- **Shopify** : Ideal for e-commerce websites, Shopify provides tools to sell products online without needing technical skills.

- **Bluehost** : With Bluehost web hosting, you get all the features, tools, and guidance you need to build and launch awe-inspiring WordPress websites.

- **NameCheap:** Gives feature-filled, cost-effective website hosting solutions with plans to suit businesses of all sizes. You can quickly build your site code-free with its customizable templates and drag-and-drop editor and get a custom email address for professional use.

Each platform comes with templates and easy-to-use interfaces, so you can create a website that reflects your brand without any coding knowledge.

There are a lot of different services, so shop around. Cost can vary; hosting service can start at @1.99 to 149.99. It is a big stretch, but it depends on your needs. If you are selling a product, Shopify is highly recommended. Hostinger, Bluehost, or WIX are good places to start if you don't need e-commerce services.

AI your Website & Content Creator

ChatGPT can be a powerful tool for website creation by streamlining the creativity, design, and content creation processes. It can assist in generating ideas for the site's structure, recommending design layouts, and suggesting the best platforms to use based on your needs. Natural language interaction helps break down complex technical aspects into simple, understandable terms, making them accessible to non-developers.

Once the framework is established, ChatGPT can be leveraged to write content for the site, such as crafting engaging landing page copy, product descriptions, or blog posts. This is particularly beneficial for those who struggle with content creation, as the tool can generate SEO-friendly text and adapt its style based on the tone you want for your website. Additionally, it can help optimize the website for search engines by suggesting appropriate meta descriptions, keywords, and headlines.

Finally, ChatGPT can also assist in troubleshooting and customizing elements as your website as it evolves. It can be a versatile partner throughout the website creation process, from offering recommendations on user experience improvements to providing code snippets for minor customizations (like embedding forms or tweaking visual elements). Ultimately, ChatGPT allows you to focus on the creative and strategic aspects of building a website while handling much of the technical work.

Pro tip:

With more people browsing the web on their phones, ensuring your website is mobile-friendly is critical. Luckily, most website builders automatically optimize templates for mobile. Make sure this option is available.

The Phone Service, CRM, and the Gmail Mirage: Unveiling the Secrets to Business Success

The Business Line

First impressions matter, especially in the business world. Having a separate phone line for your business immediately projects professionalism and credibility. When potential clients or customers see a dedicated business number, you are serious about your venture and committed to providing exceptional service. It instills confidence and sets the stage for positive interactions.

A separate phone line allows you to provide dedicated customer service separate from your calls. By having a designated line solely for business-related inquiries, you can prioritize and respond promptly to customer needs. This level of attentiveness demonstrates your commitment to exceptional customer service, fostering trust and loyalty among your clientele. It also ensures that personal and business calls do not mix, avoiding potential confusion or unprofessional interactions.

Starting a new business can be all-consuming, often blurring the lines between work and personal life. Having a separate phone line allows you to establish boundaries and maintain a healthier work-life balance. By switching off your business line after business hours, you can recharge and focus on personal matters without being constantly tied to work-related calls. This separation can help prevent burnout and ensure you have the time and energy to devote to your business and personal well-being.

Many options exist for starting a new phone service without breaking the bank. Here are three services that start for as little as $10. Here are a couple of services that you can check out:

Google Voice: Business Phone System: As of 10/24/24, plans start at $10 monthly. They integrate desktop and mobile apps, so there is no need for an additional phone. They offer unlimited domestic calling and text messaging. (https://workspace.google.com/products/voice/)

Vonage Business Service: As of 10/24/24, plans start at $13.99 monthly. They integrate desktop and mobile apps, so there is no need for an additional phone. They offer unlimited domestic calling and text messaging. (https://www.vonage.com/unified-communications/small-business/plans-and-pricing/)

THE CRM: Your Secret Weapon for Success

Using a CRM (Customer Relationship Management) system can be a game-changer for small businesses, startups, or entrepreneurs looking to manage customer interactions, sales, and marketing efforts without incurring significant costs. What a CRM does is streamline processes and enhance customer relationships. Here's a look at the benefits, limitations, and popular options when using a free CRM.

How the CRM will organize your business

1. **Centralized Customer Data** : A CRM helps store and organize customer contact details, communication history, and notes, giving you a clear overview of each customer or lead. Managing follow-ups, personalizing

interactions, and maintaining relationships becomes easier with all the information in one place.

2. **Automated Sales and Marketing Processes** : CRMs often include features like email marketing automation, task reminders, and pipeline management to help track where your leads are in the sales process. Automating routine tasks allows you to focus on more strategic activities, such as closing deals or nurturing high-value prospects.

3. **Team Collaboration** : CRMs allow multiple users to access and share information for businesses with small teams. This ensures everyone is on the same page and can work collaboratively, improving productivity and communication within the team. Even if there is no team yet, bringing a person on board will make it easier to help keep customers happy.

4. **Cost-Effective Growth** : Many CRM tools offer excellent options for new businesses with limited budgets. They allow you to manage customer relationships and sales processes without the upfront cost of a premium solution. Many CRMs offer scalable plans as your business grows, enabling you to upgrade only when necessary.

Limitations of a Free CRM

While free CRMs offer many benefits, they also come with certain limitations that may restrict functionality as your business grows:

1. **Limited Features** : Free versions often come with essential features and may lack advanced capabilities like custom reporting, integrations with third-party tools, or enhanced automation features.

2. **User Restrictions** : CRMs have user limits, meaning only a small number of team members can access the system.

3. **Storage and Contact Limits** : Free CRMs often restrict the number of contacts or records you can store and the amount of data you can upload. If you have a large customer base, this might not be sufficient in the long run.

4. **Limited Support** : Free CRMs may not offer the same level of customer support as paid versions. If you run into technical issues or need help optimizing your CRM, you might have to rely on community forums or online documentation rather than dedicated support.

Popular Free CRM Options

1. **HubSpot CRM** : One of the most popular free CRMs, HubSpot offers a wide range of features, including contact management, email tracking, and sales pipelines. It is user-friendly, integrates with many third-party tools, and has no user or storage limits.

2. **ZohoCRM** : Zoho's free plan offers essential CRM features, including lead management, task automation, and basic reporting for up to 3 users. It's a good option for small businesses looking for a simple, easy-to-use CRM.

3. **Bitrix24** : Bitrix24 offers a free CRM with up to 12 users, making it suitable for small teams. It includes contact management, sales tracking, project management, and social media integrations, although some advanced features are reserved for paid plans.

4. **Freshsales (Freshworks)** : Freshsales provides a free CRM option tailored for small businesses. The plan includes basic sales pipelines and workflows and offers contact and lead management, email tracking, and integrations with other Freshworks products.

5. **Agile CRM** : Agile CRM provides a free plan for up to 10 users and offers features like contact

management, email marketing, and appointment scheduling. It also supports task automation and integrates with third-party tools.

A CRM is an excellent way to organize customer data, manage leads, and improve communication without a significant financial investment. While free CRMs have limitations, they can be sufficient for small businesses or entrepreneurs starting. As your business grows and your needs become more complex, most CRM platforms offer flexible, scalable options to upgrade.

Free Email vs Paid Email: The Limitations of Free Gmail for Business Use

While Gmail is a fantastic tool for personal communication, using it as your primary email platform for business purposes has limitations. Gmail lacks the advanced features necessary for efficient business communication. You deserve more than just a cluttered inbox and scattered conversations. A dedicated business email service enhances your professionalism. It offers features like advanced contact management, automated workflows, and insightful analytics, allowing you to stay organized and focused on growing your business.

Professional communication mediums are critical in shaping your brand's professionalism and credibility. Understanding the differences between free and domain-based email accounts, the importance of a dedicated business phone number, and the advantages of virtual numbers can significantly impact how clients perceive your business.

Free email accounts often lack the credibility associated with domain-based emails. When potential clients see a generic email address like yourname@gmail.com, it may not instill confidence in your business' legitimacy. In contrast, an email from a custom domain, such as yourname@yourbusiness.com, projects a sense of professionalism and commitment. It shows that you have invested in establishing a formal communication channel, thus boosting client trust.

Security is another critical aspect where free email accounts fall short compared to domain-based emails. Free services are typically more susceptible to spam and security risks, making them less reliable for professional use. In contrast, domain-based emails often come with enhanced security features such as two-factor authentication and data encryption, offering better protection against cyber threats. This added layer of security ensures that sensitive communications remain private and secure.

A dedicated business phone number is valuable for maintaining professionalism and operational efficiency. Separating personal and professional calls creates a clear boundary that helps manage work-life balance. This separation also ensures that all business communications receive the appropriate attention and response time, reinforcing a professional image. Furthermore, using a dedicated business number makes tracking and managing client interactions easier, which is essential for providing consistent and reliable customer service.

Lastly, setting up a business email gives you access to support. If your email has an issue, you can reach out to someone for help. That is worth its weight in gold. There are so many options to choose from. Getting a business email is affordable and can be purchased at most the hosting site. You can set it up where you bought your domain name.

Choosing Platforms for Selling

Once you know where your audience spends time, it's important to decide which platforms to use to sell your products or services; platforms focusing on product discovery, shopping features, and advertising are ideal for driving sales. Visual content is key here, as it draws in potential customers and helps them connect with your brand:

- **Instagram:** A visual platform that allows you to use shoppable posts, stories, and Reels to highlight your products.

- **Facebook:** With features like Facebook Shops and Marketplace, this platform enables direct sales and integrates well with targeted advertising.

- **Pinterest:** Known for its focus on creativity and inspiration, it is perfect for showcasing products people seek.

- **TikTok:** A fast-growing platform that allows you to create short, engaging videos to attract attention and drive sales, especially to a younger audience.

Knowing your goals can better tailor your social media efforts to meet your business needs.

Researching Your Audience

Understanding who your audience is and how they use social media is crucial for success. Every platform caters to different demographics, and your choice should align with where your customers spend their time. Here to consider when researching your audience:

- **Age:** Different age groups gravitate toward different platforms. For example, Instagram and TikTok are popular among younger users (ages 18-34), while Facebook tends to attract an older demographic (30+).
- **Interests:** What are your audience's hobbies, preferences, and needs? Knowing this will help you craft content that resonates with them.
- **Buying behavior:** What platforms do they use when they are ready to purchase? Instagram and Facebook create powerful shopping ads and influencer collaboration opportunities.
- **Engagement style:** Some audiences prefer real-time communication, while others prefer platforms that allow them to browse content at their own pace.

Maximizing Social Media for Sales and Relationships

Social media is one of the most powerful tools for business marketing today, allowing you to connect with your audience and increase sales. However, choosing the right platforms based on your specific business goals is essential to maximize its potential. The key to success is knowing which platforms to focus on to sell your products and which to use to build lasting customer relationships.

Defining Your Business Goals

Before diving into social media marketing, the first step is to define your goals. Are you looking to generate direct sales or more focused on building a community and fostering relationships? Sales-oriented platforms help you reach new customers and convert them into buyers, while relationship-driven platforms allow for more personal interaction, which can lead to long-term loyalty.

Choosing Platforms for Relationship Building

Building a solid relationship with your audience helps cultivate loyalty, which can lead to repeat customers and word-of-mouth referrals. Some platforms are better suited for creating these connections, as they allow more personal interaction and engagement:

- **LinkedIn** is a professional networking platform suitable for business-to-business (B2B) relationships. It allows you to establish thought leadership and connect with other professionals.

- **Facebook:** Community groups enable you to build close-knit communities where customers can ask questions, share experiences, and feel connected to your brand.

- **YouTube:** Video content allows you to share in-depth stories, tutorials, or behind-the-scenes content, helping to create a strong sense of connection with your audience.

- **Twitter (now X):** This platform, known for real-time communication, allows you to interact with customers directly, answer questions, and share updates.

Tailoring Your Content to the Platform

To get the most out of each platform, it is essential to tailor your content to its audience and features. For platforms where your goal is to sell, focus on creating visually appealing, engaging content that highlights your products and encourages immediate action. For relationship-building platforms, share stories, engage in conversations, and provide valuable content that nurtures your connection with your audience.

By balancing content that drives sales with content that builds relationships, you can create a dynamic and engaging social media presence that supports your business goals.

Measuring Performance and Adjusting

Success on social media doesn't happen overnight. It's essential to monitor your performance and adjust your strategy regularly. Track metrics like conversion rates, clicks, and purchases for sales-oriented platforms. For relationship-building platforms, focus on engagement metrics such as likes, comments, shares, and interactions. By continually evaluating these results, you can fine-tune your approach and ensure that your social media marketing efforts remain effective.

Audience Research Breakdown for Social Media

When researching your audience for social media marketing, consider these factors:

- **Demographics:**
    - **Instagram and TikTok:** Mostly Gen Z and Millennials (ages 18-34).
    - **Facebook:** Skews are older and popular with people aged 30+.
    - **LinkedIn:** Primarily used by professionals, ideal for B2B services.
    - **Pinterest:** Dominantly female audience, popular with DIY, fashion, and home décor enthusiasts.
- **Engagement Habits:**
    - **Instagram and Pinterest:** Users are drawn to visually engaging content ideal for selling products.
    - **Facebook and LinkedIn:** More suited for community engagement, discussions, and professional networking.

- **Purchase Behavior:**
    - **Instagram, Facebook, and TikTok:** High shopping activity, primarily through ads and influencers.
    - **Pinterest:** Users are actively looking for products and ideas to purchase.

By understanding the audience's preferences and habits, you can effectively tailor your content and strategy to meet their needs. With the right approach, social media can be a powerful tool for growing sales and relationships, helping you build a robust and lasting business. Do not overwhelm yourself. Pick out 1-3 platforms and learn how they work. Check your competitors to see what works and what does not.

Leveraging Social Media Quickly

Getting up to speed

To quickly learn a social media platform for business, start by setting clear goals, such as increasing brand awareness or driving sales. Explore tutorials, online courses, or YouTube videos to understand the platform's features. Study how competitors use the platform, paying attention to the types of content they post and what engages their audience. Use the platform to experiment with different content formats, hashtags, and ads. Stay updated on trends and best practices by following social media marketing experts and joining online communities where businesses share tips and strategies. This approach will help you efficiently master the platform for business use.

Automating your post

Also, when you are ready to begin posting, consider using a social media scheduler. A scheduler can set up your post ideas days or even weeks ahead. Canva is an excellent option. Canva simplifies social media posting by offering customizable templates optimized for each platform, ensuring consistent branding with saved fonts, colors, and logos. It allows users to create eye-catching posts using its drag-and-drop editor, access millions of stock images, and even design videos or GIFs. With Canva Pro, you can schedule and publish content directly to your accounts, collaborate with team members, and track performance with built-in analytics, making it an all-in-one tool for creating and managing social media content.

Scaling Your Business with Affiliate Marketing: A Low-Cost Strategy

Integrating affiliate marketing into your business provides an effective route to increasing revenue streams without high upfront costs or extensive product development. This approach is especially beneficial for women entrepreneurs who manage small or home-based businesses, as it allows them to leverage existing products and services to generate steady income through commissions. By partnering with affiliates who can promote their offerings, these entrepreneurs can enhance their business growth and profitability while maintaining flexibility and managing fewer complexities.

How Affiliate Marketing Can Complement Your Business

Affiliate marketing is an effective way to enhance your business by leveraging the reach and influence of others to drive sales. By partnering with affiliates, you tap into new audiences who might not have discovered your products or services. This expanded reach can significantly increase your brand visibility and lead to higher sales, all while keeping marketing costs low since you only pay affiliates when they deliver tangible results.

Additionally, affiliate marketing can strengthen your brand's credibility. Affiliates often promote your business through their established platforms, and their endorsement can be a powerful form of social proof. Potential customers who see your products recommended by a trusted source can lead to a positive cycle where increased trust increases sales, attracting more affiliates to your program.

Moreover, affiliate marketing offers valuable insights into your customers' behavior. The data collected from affiliate campaigns can help you understand which strategies are working and where improvements can be made. This allows you to fine-tune your marketing efforts and focus on the tactics that generate the best results, making your overall marketing strategy more efficient and effective.

Selecting the Right Affiliate Programs and Promoting Offers on Various Platforms

The key to Affiliate marketing is partnering with the right affiliate and getting them to partner with you. As you look for the right affiliate, you will find some are harder to partner with than others. Some only work with established businesses, while others are more lenient. Pay also differs between affiliates. Be very strategic in the companies you partner with. You don't want to promote a company with a bad or questionable reputation. The old saying goes, "All money isn't good money." Be protective of your business reputation.

Promoting affiliate products can significantly boost your sales by diversifying your income streams and broadening your product range. By offering affiliate products alongside your own, you can generate additional revenue without the need for extra inventory or operational costs. This allows you to cater to a broader audience and meet more of their needs, which can lead to increased sales overall.

Incorporating affiliate products into your business strategy enhances your credibility and fosters trust with your audience. When you recommend quality products that align with your brand, customers will likely view you as a reliable source of information and value. This trust can translate into higher sales for affiliate products and your offerings, as customers are more inclined to purchase from someone they trust.

Affiliate marketing provides cross-promotion and content marketing opportunities, which can drive more traffic to your site. Creating content around affiliate products, such as reviews or tutorials, can improve your website's SEO and attract organic traffic. This increased visibility not only boosts sales of the affiliate products but also enhances the likelihood that customers will explore and purchase your products, leading to overall growth in your business.

Building Trust & Leading

When integrating affiliate marketing into a business, selecting effective affiliate programs and leveraging multiple promotional platforms are crucial to maximizing monetization opportunities. This section will explore evaluating affiliate programs, choosing the right affiliates, utilizing various promotional platforms effectively, and tracking performance to optimize campaigns.

A business must start by evaluating affiliate programs based on several critical factors. One of the primary considerations is the commission structure. The commission structure should provide a fair and motivating incentive for affiliates while ensuring it remains sustainable for your business. Different commission structures have advantages and drawbacks, such as tiered, recurring, or one-time commissions. For instance, recurring commissions can offer ongoing passive income but may require more complex tracking mechanisms. Ensuring that the selected program aligns with your financial model is essential in fostering long-term success.

Next, the relevancy of the affiliate program to your niche is paramount. Affiliates promoting products or services like yours are more likely to understand your market and audience preferences. This alignment can enhance the credibility of your offers and increase conversion rates. Additionally, assessing the quality of the affiliate network itself is necessary. Reputable affiliate networks usually provide robust tracking, reporting tools, and fraud prevention measures that protect affiliates and merchants from potential pitfalls.

After identifying promising affiliate programs, the next step is to research and choose affiliates that share your target audience and have a proven track record of successful promotions. Finding affiliates with an established audience in your niche can result in more meaningful engagements and higher conversion rates. Look for affiliates who create quality content, maintain strong relationships with their followers, and demonstrate authenticity in their promotions. Tools like affiliate marketplaces and influencer databases can help identify potential partners whose audiences align well with yours. Check out some well-known affiliate programs:

CJ:

https://www.cj.com/

Share a Sale:

https://www.shareasale.com/

eBay:

https://partnernetwork.ebay.com/

Walmart:

https://creator.walmart.com/

ClickBank :

https://www.clickbank.com/

There are thousands of affiliate programs to choose from. Typically, when going to the bottom of a website, you will see a reference to the affiliate program. Equally important is the method of promotion. Utilizing different platforms can vastly improve the outreach and effectiveness of affiliate marketing efforts. Social media, blogs, and email marketing are the most influential channels for promoting affiliate offers.

Social media provides a real-time platform to engage with audiences and share content. When using social media, consistency is vital. Regular posts, stories, and updates keep interest alive and drive traffic to your affiliate links. Each social media platform has unique strengths; for example, Instagram can be particularly effective for product-based promotions due to its visual nature, while LinkedIn might be better suited for B2B services.

Blogs allow you to create in-depth content around your affiliate products or services. Writing honest reviews, how-to guides, and case studies can establish your authority in the niche and provide value to your readers. Integrating affiliate links within such content makes it more organic and less intrusive, enhancing user trust and increasing conversion rates.

Email marketing remains one of the most powerful tools in digital marketing. Building an email list gives you direct access to an interested audience. Segmenting your email list allows personalized communication, significantly boosting engagement and sales. Promotional emails, newsletters, and exclusive deals sent through emails can drive substantial traffic to your affiliate links.

Tracking and analyzing performance metrics is crucial to optimizing affiliate campaigns and ensuring maximum return on investment (ROI). Implementing advanced tracking tools enables businesses to monitor the effectiveness of various affiliates and advertising strategies. Metrics such as click-through rates (CTR), conversion rates, average order value (AOV), and overall revenue generated from affiliate links provide valuable insights into what is working and what needs improvement.

Regular analysis of these metrics helps in making informed decisions. For example, if a specific affiliate drives high traffic but low conversions, it might indicate the need to adjust its promotional strategy or provide better incentives. On the other hand, affiliates with high conversion rates can be given additional support and resources to maximize their impact further.

Test different strategies and vary your promotional tactics to find the optimal mix. A/B testing can be beneficial in determining the best approaches for various segments of your audience. Continually optimizing campaigns ensures they remain effective and profitable over time.

Your Business Blueprint: Key Steps for Online Success

Establishing a solid online persona can set the foundation for business growth and credibility, sparking interest and trust among potential clients and stakeholders. Throughout this book, I have explored various strategies and tools that will empower you to design an impactful online presence tailored to your unique business needs. Designing a solid online presence will strengthen your business in the real world.

Your journey toward creating a noteworthy business begins with understanding your brand identity. Defining your mission, values, and unique selling proposition (USP) is fundamental. This core groundwork will guide every subsequent decision, from choosing the right social media platforms to developing a cohesive visual aesthetic that resonates with your target audience. Your brand must speak volumes and reflect authenticity and professionalism.

Social media remains an indispensable tool for modern entrepreneurs. Strategically scheduling posts, engaging with followers, and sharing valuable content helps build a community around your brand. Nevertheless, it's vital to remain authentic and personal; people connect with people, not faceless companies. Regularly responding to comments, sharing behind-the-scenes glimpses, and showing appreciation for your followers' support humanizes your brand.

Investing time creating a user-friendly website is the cornerstone of your online presence. Your website should be easy to navigate, aesthetically pleasing, and filled with valuable information. Integrating a blog can further enhance your credibility, showcase your expertise, and provide value to your readers. Moreover, search engine optimization (SEO) practices are crucial here—ensuring your site appears in relevant searches will increase visibility and drive traffic.

A business email is essential for building trust and credibility with clients and partners. It demonstrates professionalism by showing that you are committed to your business, setting you apart from those who use generic email services like Gmail or Yahoo. A branded email also reinforces your business identity, contributing to more robust brand recognition whenever you communicate. Additionally, business emails are more secure, giving clients peace of mind that their information is handled safely. Ultimately, using a business email boosts customer confidence, as it conveys legitimacy and stability, making your business appear more established and trustworthy.

Establishing partnerships, affiliate partnerships, and collaborations can further amplify your reach. Networking with fellow entrepreneurs and influencers in your field can open doors to broader audiences. Guest blogging, co-hosting webinars, and participating in virtual events are excellent ways to gain exposure while sharing knowledge and learning from others.

A strategic approach to budgeting includes leveraging free resources and tools initially. Many robust platforms offer free versions that can effectively serve new or small businesses. As your business grows, you can upgrade to premium versions that provide additional features. Always question the necessity and expected outcome before committing significant funds to any new tool or service.

To consolidate what has been discussed throughout this book, here is a comprehensive checklist that will help ensure you cover all aspects of building a professional online presence:

1. **Define Your Brand Identity**
   - Mission Statement
   - Core Values
   - Unique Selling Proposition (USP)

2. **Select Appropriate Social Media Platforms**
   - Identify where your target audience spends time
   - Develop a content calendar
   - Engage consistently with followers

3. **Design a User-Friendly Website**
   - Ensure easy navigation and aesthetic appeal
   - Include essential pages: Home, About, Services/Products, Contact
   - Implement Search Engine Optimization (SEO)

4. **Start a Blog**
   - Plan topics relevant to your audience
   - Write consistently and share expertise
   - Promote blog posts through social media and email

- A great way to show uses affiliate partners to engage and make money

1. **Utilize Email Marketing**
    - Build an email list
    - Create engaging newsletters with exclusive content
    - Personalize emails to foster connection

1. **Network and Collaborate**
    - Seek out partnerships with similar businesses
    - Participate in virtual events, webinars, and guest blogging
    - Share knowledge and learnings
    - Create a strong affiliate network to build creditability to sell and introduce your products.

1. **Stay Budget-Conscious**
    - Begin with free or low-cost tools
    - Evaluate expenditures regularly

- Prioritize investments aligned with business goals

1. **Constantly Analyze and Improve**
    - Monitor analytics for social media, website, and email campaigns
    - Adjust strategies based on performance data
    - Stay updated with industry trends and adapt accordingly

Final Thoughts and Gratitude

Dear Reader,

Congratulations on reading The Digital Startup Playbook: Your First Steps to Online Success! I hope you've found value in these pages and that they've given you the tools and confidence to embark on your online business journey.

Building something from the ground up is never easy, but remember—every successful business begins with a single step. You've already taken the first step. Remember, it is not where you start but where you end.

There will be doubt, challenges, and perhaps even a few setbacks. But don't lose sight of the incredible vision you have. Keep pushing forward, stay committed, and trust in your abilities to overcome whatever obstacles may come.

The path to success is rarely straightforward, but your determination and passion will guide you. With each step, you're building something for today, your future, and the legacy you'll leave behind. Keep your eyes on the prize.

I wish you the very best of luck on your journey! May this playbook serve as a source of inspiration and a guide as you continue to build the business of your dreams.

To your success,
Cheronda Maccanico-Shepherd

www.ingramcontent.com/pod-product-compliance
Lightning Source LLC
Chambersburg PA
CBHW062123220526
45471CB00010B/3859